TAXES FOR KIDS

LEARN HOW TAXES HELP
THE WORLD

BY

CA ANSHUL KARWA

Table of Contents

No part of this book can be reproduced in any form whatsoever without the prior approval of the author. The information contained in this book is for educational purposes only.

The information contained in this book has been compiled from sources deemed reliable, and it is accurate to the best of author's knowledge, however, the author cannot guarantee its accuracy and validity and cannot be held liable for any errors or omissions.

Thank You Note

This book is dedicated to all the amazing teachers and parents who help or assist us study and learn new things every day.

To all the wonderful and amazing teachers, thank you for your patience, guidance, and for making learning fun to all kids around the world. You've shown them the importance of knowledge, and every grown up wouldn't be anything without you.

And to my dear parents, thank you for your endless love, support, and for always believing in me. You taught me the values of kindness and hard work, and I'm forever grateful.

This book is for you, with all my respect and love!

ABOUT THE AUTHOR

Hi, I'm Anshul Karwa, a Chartered Accountant who loves making complex topics easy and fun for everyone, including kids! With additional qualifications in law and computer applications, I bring a solid mix of finance, legal and technical skills to everything I do.

With more than nine years of experience on the stock market, I have been in bear and bull markets, learning valuable lessons along the way. My journey gave me a deeper understanding of economic development and how to see opportunities where others might see challenges.

During my corporate career, I've worked with multinational companies like Deloitte and JSW. These studies have formed my economic insights and hassle fixing talents, getting ready me to proportion that know how with young minds.

My Mission:

My aim is to help youngsters like you to recognize the sector of taxes with my book, "Taxes for Kids: Learn how taxes help the sector" Through simple tales, sensible examples, and amusing sports, I want to expose how taxes work and why they depend. I hope to guide young readers closer to becoming smart, informed citizens of the destiny.

Introduction

What is Tax?

Imagine you have a piggy bank, and every time you buy a toy or a candy, you put a small coin in it. That coin is like a tax. Just like your piggy bank helps you save money to buy something bigger later, the government collects taxes from people to build things like schools, parks, roads, and hospitals.

Have you ever wondered how a government school was built or who pays for the roads your school bus travels on? Well, that's where something called "tax" comes in!

Let's understand with a fun story!

Imagine you, Ria, and Aarav are playing in a park. You all love the swings and slides, but one day, you notice the swings are broken! Who's going to fix them?

The park doesn't have a magic repairman who works for free. Instead, your parents, and all the other grown-ups, give a little bit of their money to the government. This money is called a "tax." The government then uses this tax money to fix the swings, build new slides, and make sure the park stays clean and fun for everyone.

Another example:

Let's say Rishabh buys a chocolate bar from the store. The store owner tells her the chocolate costs 10, but she has to pay 12. Why? Because that extra 2 is a small tax that goes to the government. With this tax money, the government can build new schools, hospitals, and even roads to make sure you can get to the store to buy more chocolate!

So, **tax** is like a tiny piece of everyone's money that helps make sure our parks, schools, and roads are in good shape. Without taxes, we wouldn't have these things!

Why This Book?

Hey kids! Have you ever wondered why grown-ups talk about taxes? You might have heard your parents or teachers mention it, and maybe you thought, "What's the big deal?"

Let's find out together!

Imagine Rohan and Meera are curious kids just like you. One day, they asked their parents, "Why do we pay taxes?" But the answers were a bit tricky to understand. Taxes sounded like a big, complicated thing that only grown-ups needed to worry about.

But guess what? Understanding taxes isn't that hard, and it's actually pretty cool! This book is here to help kids like Rohan, Meera, and you understand what taxes are and why they're important. We'll take you on a fun adventure to learn how taxes help build the things you love, like your school, the roads you travel on, and even the park where you play.

Why should you read this book?

Because learning about taxes now will make you super smart! When you grow up, you'll know exactly how things work and why it's important to share and help out, just like your parents do. Plus, you'll be able to teach other kids too!

So, let's explore the world of taxes together! It's not just for grown-ups—it's for curious kids like you!

Chapter 1: Why Do We Pay Taxes?

The Role of the Government

Let's imagine you and your friends, Ishaan and Priya, are playing a game. In this game, someone has to be the leader or monitor who makes sure everyone is playing fair, that the rules are followed, and that everyone is having fun. In actual life if we see, that leader or monitor is like the government.

But what does the government actually do?

The government is like a big helper for the whole country. Just like how your school has a principal to make sure everything runs smoothly, the government makes sure everything in the country works well. They help build schools, fix roads, and make sure everyone is safe and healthy.

So now your questions should be "WHY TAXES"?

So, here's where taxes come in.

Let's say Kamal's bike has a flat tire. He needs help fixing it, but fixing things costs money. The government doesn't have a magic money tree, so where do they get the money from? They get it from taxes!

A Example for you to understand:

Suppose a kid named Alia's school needs new books for the library. Now the government can buy those books because people pay taxes. So, when your parents go to work, they work and earn money, and a small part of that money goes to the government as taxes. The government then uses that money to buy books, build roads, provide safety to people and do many other important things that help every citizen of that country.

So why do our parents pay taxes?

They pay taxes to help the government take care of all of us. Taxes are like a giant and huge piggy bank that everyone adds a little bit of money to, so we can have nice things like schools, hospitals, and safe roads to travel on.

Without the government and the taxes we pay it would be really hard to keep everything running smoothly. That's why paying taxes is so important! It's how we all work together to make our country a great place to live.

why do we give money to the government?

The government is like a big family that takes care of everyone in the country. To do this, they need money, just like how your parents need money to buy food and clothes for you. Taxes are the money people give to the government to help them take care of the country and also for people who don't earn.

What happens if we don't pay taxes?

If people don't pay taxes, the government won't have enough money to fix roads, build schools, or keep us safe. That's why paying taxes is important, it helps everyone.

What Happens if We Don't Pay Taxes?

Let's imagine a fun day where you, Dhruv, and Shubham decide to have a picnic in your favorite park. You pack your snacks, toys, and head to the park, but when you get there, something's wrong. The swings are broken, the grass is overgrown, and the trash garbage is overflowing!

Why is the park in such bad shape?

Well, let's think about it. If people stop paying taxes, the government won't have enough money to fix things like the park. The money that usually goes to fixing swings, cutting the grass, or keeping the park clean comes from taxes. Without taxes, there's no money for these important jobs.

Another Example:

Payal's school bus needs a new engine so it can keep taking kids to school. But if no one pays taxes, the government can't help fix the bus. That means Payal and her friends might not be able to get to school easily.

So,

If people don't pay taxes, things in our community could start to fall apart. Schools might not have enough books, roads could get bumpy and unsafe, and parks might not be fun to play in anymore. Taxes help keep everything running smoothly, so it's important that everyone pitches in!

Chapter 2: Direct and Indirect Taxes

What are Direct Taxes?

Let's imagine your friend Aryan just got some pocket money from his parents for doing a great job on his homework. He's really excited and wants to save some of it to buy a new toy. But before he can do that, he needs to give a small part of his pocket money to the government. This small part is called a direct tax.

But how does it work in real life?

When grown-ups like your parents go to work, they earn money just like Aryan earned his pocket money. The government asks them to pay a small part of that money as tax. This is called income tax because it comes directly from the money they earn (which is called income). They don't give the money to someone else first—it goes straight to the government.

A Example:

Let's say Aryan's dad earns 100 for a day's work. Before he can spend that money, he has to give 10 to the government as income tax. This 10 is a direct tax because it goes straight from Aryan's dad to the government.

Why is this important?

Direct taxes help the government pay for important things like schools, hospitals, and roads. When everyone gives a small part of their money, it adds up to a lot, and the government can use it to take care of the country.

So, basically, Direct taxes are like a birthday gift you give directly to your friend. When grown-ups earn money, they give a part of it directly to the government as tax. This is called income tax.

So, direct taxes are like a way for grown-ups to share some of the money they earn to help make sure everyone has what they need!

What are Indirect Taxes?

Indirect taxes are a little different. Imagine you're buying ice cream, and the shopkeeper adds a small extra amount to the price. That extra amount is an indirect tax, and it goes to the government too! In your country, this is called GST (Goods and Services Tax).

Imagine you and your friend Anya are at the cafe, and Anya wants to buy her favorite chocolate pastry. The price on the shelf says 10, but when she gets to the counter, the shopkeeper says, "That will be 12." Anya wonders why the price is different.

Here's the secret: It's because of something called an indirect tax.

How does it work?

Unlike direct taxes, which are taken directly from the money people earn, indirect taxes are added to the price of things you buy. The extra 2 that Anya had to pay is an indirect tax called GST (Goods and Services Tax). The shopkeeper collects this extra money and then gives it to the government.

A Example:

Let's say your family goes out for dinner, and the bill comes to 500. But when you look closely, you see that the final bill is 550. That extra 50 is an indirect tax. It's added to the cost of your meal, and the restaurant gives it to the government.

Why do we have indirect taxes?

Indirect taxes help the government collect money without taking it directly from people's pockets. Instead, it's added to the things we buy, like chocolates, toys, or even a new pair of shoes. The government then uses this money to do important things, like fixing roads, building parks, and providing electricity.

So, every time you buy something and notice a slight increase in price, remember, the extra money is an indirect tax that helps make our country a better place to live!

Chapter 3: How Do Taxes Help Us?

Building Schools and Hospitals

Let's imagine that you, Rohan, and Aditi are super excited because a brand-new government school is being built in your neighbourhood. But have you ever wondered how the school is being built?

Here's the answer: Taxes!

So,

When your parents and other grown-ups pay taxes, the government collects that money to build schools where kids like you can learn, play, and make new friends. Taxes also help pay for teachers, books, and even the playground where you'll have fun during recess.

Understanding Government Schools and Private Schools

In every country, there are two types of schools where kids can learn: government schools and private schools. Let's learn and see what makes them both of them different from each other.

Government Schools

Government schools are like a big gift from the government to all the children in the country. These schools are built using the money from taxes that your mom and dad and also other grown up people pay. Because the government builds and runs these schools, often kids like you don't have to pay much or most of the times anything at all to study there.

But what if you don't go to a government school?

Some kids, like you, Rohan, and Aditi, might go to a private school. That's okay! Even though you don't go to a government school, it's important to know that these schools help many children whose families might not have a lot of money.

Private Schools

Private schools, on the other hand, are built and run by private groups or individuals, not the government. These schools usually have more resources like fancy classrooms, special activities, and more teachers. Because of this, parents usually pay more money for their kids to study in private schools.

But here's something really important: Even private schools help children from families who might not be able to afford the fees. In your country, private schools have to reserve some seats for kids from poorer families. This means that every child has a chance to get a good education, whether they are rich or poor.

Why Both Schools Are Important

Both government and private schools play a big role in helping children learn and grow. Government schools make sure that every child can go to school, even if their family doesn't have much money. Private schools offer different types of education, often with extra facilities and activities.

So, whether you go to a government school or a private school, remember that both are important for different reasons. And thanks to taxes, the government can build schools for everyone and help make sure that every child gets a chance to learn, no matter where they come from.

Now, what about when you're not feeling well?

If you or Aditi get a fever, you go to the government hospital to see a doctor. But hospitals don't just appear out of nowhere! They are built using the money from taxes. This money also helps pay for doctors, nurses, and all the medicine that helps you get better.

Fixing Roads and Parks

Now, imagine Rohan and Aditi are planning a bike ride to the park. But wait! What if the road to the park is full of big holes? It wouldn't be a very fun ride, right?

Here's where taxes come to the rescue!

Taxes are used to fix roads so that they are smooth and safe for everyone. That means Rohan and Aditi can ride their bikes without any bumps!

When you get to the park, you'll notice that the swings are working perfectly, the grass is cut neatly, and there's no trash lying around. All of this is possible because the government uses tax money to take care of parks, making them a fun and safe place for kids to play.

Other Ways Taxes Help

Did you know that taxes help in lots of other ways too?

- Streetlights: When you walk home in the evening, streetlights help you see where you're going. Taxes pay for those lights and keep them shining bright.

- Police and Firefighters: If there's an emergency, like a fire or someone needs help, police officers and firefighters are there to protect us. They do their important jobs thanks to the money from taxes.

- Public Libraries: Do you love reading books? Public libraries, where you can borrow books for free, are also built and maintained using tax money.

Taxes are like the glue that holds our communities together. They make sure we have schools to learn in, hospitals to keep us healthy, roads and parks to enjoy, and so much more. By paying taxes, everyone pitches in to make sure our world is a better, safer, and happier place for all of us.

Chapter 4: Preparing for Taxes

How Do Grown-Ups Pay Taxes?

You might have seen your parents sitting with papers and calculators, looking very serious. They're not doing homework, they're getting ready to pay their taxes! But how do they do it? Let's learn it step by step:

Step 1: Earning Money

First, let's imagine your friend Aarav's mom is a doctor. She works at a hospital and earns money for helping people get better. This money is called her income. Everyone who works—like teachers, shopkeepers, and drivers—earns income.

Step 2: Figuring Out the Tax

Aarav's mom knows that she needs to give a small part of her income to the government as tax. But how does she know how much to pay? That's where math comes in! Grown-ups use their income and follow special rules to figure out how much tax they owe.

But you know in practical life many times the rules can be tricky, and this is where the real heroes come in: **Chartered Accountants (CAs)**!

Step 3: The Supermen Behind Taxes

Chartered Accountants, or CAs, are like the supermen and superwomen of the tax world. They have to study really hard and pass very tough exams to become experts and even study after exams throughout the life. Not everyone can do it. They're the most respectable educated community all over the world. CAs are the ones who help people figure out how much tax to pay, making sure everything is done correctly. They know all the rules and can solve even the trickiest tax problems. So, if Aarav's mom needs help, she can go to a CA, who will help her in to save the day with their super tax powers!

Step 4: Paying the Tax

Once Aarav's mom knows how much tax she has to pay, she doesn't hand it over in cash. Instead, she fills out a special form, either on paper or online, and sends it to the government. This form shows how much money she earned and how much tax she needs to pay.

Step 5: Getting a Receipt

After Aarav's mom pays her tax, the government gives her a receipt. This receipt is like a thank-you note for doing her part to help the country. It's important because it shows that she has paid her tax and followed the rules.

Step 6: Using Tax Money

Remember, the money Aarav's mom paid in taxes doesn't just disappear. It goes into the big pot of money that the government uses to build schools, fix roads, and do all the other important things we've talked about.

Why Is This Important?

Grown ups pay taxes every year to make sure that our country stays strong and that everyone has what they need. It might seem like a lot of work, but paying taxes is a way for everyone to help out and make our community a better place. And with the help of super-smart Chartered Accountants, paying taxes becomes a lot easier!

So next time you see your parents working on their taxes, you'll know they're doing something really important for everyone, with a little help from the tax superheroes i.e. CAs!

Why Should We Be Honest?

Just like we are honest with our parents and teachers (most of the times, wink), it's also important to be honest when paying taxes. If everyone pays their fair share, the country can take care of everyone better.

Chapter 5: Fun with Taxes!
(Interactive Section)

Welcome to the fun part of the book! This chapter is full of activities that will help you learn more about taxes while having a great time. Ready? Let's go!

Tax Quiz

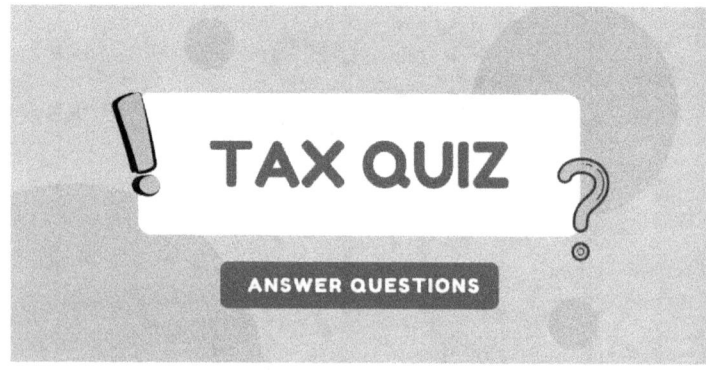

Time to test what you've learned so far! Here are some fun questions to see how much you remember. Don't worry if you don't know all the answers—you can always go back and check the previous chapters!

1. What is a direct tax?

- Is it:

a) A tax you pay when you buy something?

b) A tax that comes straight from the money people earn, like income tax?

2. What do indirect taxes help pay for?

  - Is it:

    a) The toys in the store?

    b) Things like fixing roads, building schools, and keeping parks clean?

3. Name two things taxes help build in your community.

  - Hint: Think about places where you learn, play, or travel!

4. Who are Chartered Accountants (CAs)?

  - Are they:

a) The superheroes who help people figure out and pay their taxes?

b) The people who sell chocolates at the store?

5. How do CAs help?

- Do they:

a) Make sure everyone pays the right amount of tax and follow the rules?

b) Tell you what your favorite ice cream is?

Answers:

1. A

2. B

3. Schools/Parks/Malls

4. A

5. A

Write your scores here: ____/5

Color the Tax Journey!

Get your crayons ready! Here's a fun drawing activity where you can show how taxes work.

Activity:

Color the images given in the next four pages.

I AM FUTURE
Tax Payer

TAXES FOR KIDS - CA ANSHUL KARWA

CHARTERED ACCOUNTANT SUPERHERO

CA

NAME:

Tax Maze

Help the tax payers earn Money! In this fun maze, you need to guide the tax payers from the start to the finish line. But be careful—don't take the wrong path!

Activity:

- In the next page, starting with the tax payers at the entrance.

- At the other end of the maze, guide them the correct paths without drawing in mind.

- Now, use your pencil to find the right path through the maze. Can you help the tax payers get there without getting lost?

TAX maze!

Help the businessmen find the tax!

Name _____ Age __

Bonus Activity: Tax Superhero Badge

You've learned so much about taxes—now it's time to become a Tax Superhero! We have designed a Tax Superhero Badge also you can design your own badge to show that you're a Tax Superhero who knows how important taxes are.

Activity:

- On a piece of paper, draw a big circle.

- Inside the circle, write "Tax Superhero" in big letters.

- Decorate your badge with stars, lightning bolts, or anything else that makes you feel like a superhero. Don't forget to color it in!

Fun with Friends:

Invite your friends, like Rohan, Aanya, or Aarav, to join you in these activities. You can compare your drawings, help each other with the maze, and even quiz each other on what you've learned about taxes!

Remember, learning about taxes doesn't have to be boring. With these activities, you're not just learning—you're having fun and becoming a little smarter every day!

SUMMARY: The End

Congratulations! You've made it to the end of the book. Now, let's take a moment to talk about why taxes are so important and how you, as future taxpayers, can make a big difference.

Why Taxes Are Important

Taxes are like the magic that helps make our country a better place.

Just like how you share your toys with your friends, taxes are a way grown-ups share their money to help everyone. When you grow up, you'll understand more about taxes, and you'll help make your country a great place by paying them too!

Imagine Rohan, Aanya, and Aarav sitting together in their favorite park after school. They start talking about all the things they love in their neighborhood. Rohan mentions the fun swings and slides in the park, Aanya talks about how much she enjoys learning new things at school, and Aarav is excited about the new library where he can borrow his favorite storybooks.

But then Aanya asks, "How does all of this happen? Who makes sure we have schools, parks, and libraries?" That's when Rohan's mom explains something really important: "All of these things are possible because of taxes."

Taxes are like a magic ingredient that helps our country grow and thrive. When people like your parents pay taxes, that money is used by the government to build schools where you can learn, hospitals where doctors help people get better, roads that are safe to drive on, and parks where you can play. Without taxes, many of these things wouldn't be possible.

But it's not just about building things. Taxes also help keep everything running smoothly. For example, when a road gets damaged, the government uses tax money to fix it so that everyone can travel safely. When new books are needed in the library, taxes help buy them so that you and your friends can keep reading and learning.

So, the next time you're enjoying a day at the park, studying at government school, or visiting a library, remember that taxes are behind it all, making sure you have everything you need to learn, play, and grow.

A Message for the Future Taxpayers

Now, let's think about the future. One day, when you're all grown up, you'll be earning money just like your parents do. And guess what? You'll also be paying taxes.

But don't worry, paying taxes isn't just about giving money to the government. It's about contributing to something bigger. By paying taxes, you'll be helping to build new schools for kids like you, hospitals to take care of everyone, and roads that connect all the places you need to go.

You'll also be helping to create a safe and happy community where everyone can live a good life. Whether it's making sure there are streetlights at night, keeping the parks clean, or even helping the police do their job, your taxes will make all of this possible.

Think of yourself as a superhero! Just like you learned earlier about how Chartered

Accountants are the supermen and superwomen behind taxes, you'll be a hero too, helping to build a better future for everyone.

So, as you grow up, remember that paying taxes is an important responsibility. It's your way of giving back to the community and making sure that everyone has what they need. When you become a taxpayer, you'll be playing a big part in keeping your neighbourhood, your city, and your country strong and healthy.

Author Remarks

CA ANSHUL KARWA

In Closing...

As future taxpayers, you have the power to make a real difference. Every money you contribute will help build a brighter future for your family, your friends, and everyone around you. So keep learning, keep asking questions, and always remember how important taxes are in making the world a better place.

And who knows? Maybe one day you'll even become a Chartered Accountant, helping others understand and pay their taxes, just like the superheroes you read about in this book!

All the best for your future.

-

CA ANSHUL KARWA

You can contact me at **caanshul@mail.ca.in** for further information or to discuss your specific needs. I look forward to the opportunity to help lil kids like you!

Links to my social media accounts:

- https://in.linkedin.com/in/anshulkarwa
- https://www.quora.com/profile/Anshul-Karwa
- https://www.instagram.com/anshulkarwa/
- https://twitter.com/ianshulk

Author: CA ANSHUL KARWA